THINGS LEFT UNSAID

Rosabelle Boswell

Langaa Research & Publishing CIG
Mankon, Bamenda

Publisher:
Langaa RPCIG
Langaa Research & Publishing Common Initiative Group
P.O. Box 902 Mankon
Bamenda
North West Region
Cameroon
Langaagrp@gmail.com
www.langaa-rpcig.net

Distributed in and outside N. America by African Books Collective
orders@africanbookscollective.com
www.africanbookscollective.com

ISBN-10: 9956-551-02-3

ISBN-13: 978-9956-551-02-6

The cover image is by Senzo Xulu, Nelson Mandela University. It is from the
Faculty of Arts Project, entitled the Doek Project that offered a transcription of key
arguments in doctoral theses written in isiXhosa into designer headscarves with
motifs, words, symbols relating to the subject matter investigated. It speaks to the
possibilities of border crossing in the intellectual and cultural senses, the reality of
multi-modal and multiply-situated existence and expression.

About the Poet

Rosabelle Boswell was born in Mauritius, grew up in Malawi and lives in South Africa. She is an anthropologist and author. She is author of *Le Malaise Creole: Ethnic Identity in Mauritius* (Oxford: Berghahn), *Representing Heritage in Zanzibar and Madagascar* (Addis Ababa: Eclipse); *Challenges to Identifying and Managing Intangible Cultural Heritage in Mauritius, Zanzibar and Seychelles* (Dakar: Codesria) and *Postcolonial African Anthropologies* (coedited with F. Nyamnjoh Pretoria: HSRC Press). She has also authored academic articles on cultural identity and has done ethnographic fieldwork in South Africa, Mauritius, Zanzibar, Seychelles and Madagascar. In 2010, she served as a research team leader for the Mauritius Truth and Justice Commission, examining the legacies of slavery. From 2015-2019 she was a Dean of Arts at Mandela University in South Africa.

Table of Contents

Introduction

Belonging is becoming an increasingly rare commodity in South Africa. The sense of dis-belonging is especially acute among Africans born outside of South Africa, as they experience varying levels of marginalization, including xenophobia. Some say that xenophobia is on the rise because of the legacy of racism and persistent strongholds of racial privilege. This collection of poems considers my experiences as an immigrant woman in South Africa, showing that as an ordinary human being, I am aware of the diversity of human identity, its contingency and its incompleteness. To me, identity is located in various spaces and in a diversity of experiences. The poems (*The Outsider's Gift and Blackish Woman*) reveal what it is like to live with marginality and the violence of xenophobia. These poems show that racial violence is both cognitive and visceral. The collection also highlights intimate natural spaces (*Colour, Sunshine, Ode to Rain, Holding my Mother's Hand*) that produce an ecologically embedded, oceanic (*Grounding* and *Zanzibar*) belonging. Other poems still such as *Ti La Soif* and *Manz la Caz* evoke my culinary roots and the routes that language provides in a multilingual world. In *Dust Shall Rise, True* and *Ropes* the fundamental connectivity of all those whose ancestors are from Africa – and the problem of not recognizing those fundamental and historical ties, are surfaced. These poems make specific reference to 'cords lie freshly beating still', which signal the vitality and connection of all Africans to the soil. Cords are juxtaposed to 'ropes' of slavery and bondage, and become the only conduit left for communication between Africa and the diaspora. In *If*, I evoke the desire to escape categorization, for humans to run freely beyond conventions and impositions finding solace in Western art and globally recognized literature – spaces of other complexities and which colonized people often refer to, when they seek to position themselves as members of the literate class.

Some of the poems reflect on everyday gendered impositions, places where women are forced to belong as well as belonging in locales with similarly stringent borders and requirements (*The Twatterly Twit, Zombie, Expectations*). Beyond such spaces, there are tendrils of hope (*Be Yourself Little Kite*) and the frenzy of dream crushing storms (*Little Kite and Butterfly*).

In sum, the poems show that immigrant identity is more expansive, latticed and nuanced than what we might imagine. There are many spaces and places in which ordinary human beings experience belonging and dis-belonging. Like born and bred South Africans, immigrants also find belonging in the family context, the backyard, language, the meeting, familiar landscapes and dreams. I think that South Africans might only achieve true freedom from the tyranny of singular narratives of belonging when they recognize that they too, are incomplete and have to constitute their identity continuously. Far from being a process of deprivation and lack, making identity is an enriching process that makes the world a better place. Reflecting on the process of writing these poems, I can say that I am no longer a furious writer. I am carried by words. They play in the most unexpected places. They are beautiful and I am free.

Ode to Rain

Rain, how sweet you are
We have forgotten your sullen thunder
Your rivulets writhing along pathways
the cold air you leave upon our window ledges
and the spitting stings you inflict upon our heads
Welcome back rain. We missed you.

When you are in a drought the return of rain is the sweetest blessing, even if it is violent.

Who can describe the form and depth of love one has for a mother?

Holding my Mother's hand

In the vastness of the church
I held your hand
The softness of your skin
Embracing mine
I had only that moment
Of stillness with you
But in my memory
I will hold your hand
For all time.

Grounding

Ground yourself they say. Don't be so unsettled.
However, they don't ask, were you born on sea? Did the
sea teach you how to be?
Did the Ocean teach you its vastness, its boundlessness
Did the fish show you their diversity, their mutability?
Or, are you like the monsoon that waxes with the
seasons?
Do you yearn for the deepest blue of the oceans, that
unfathomable colour of stillness?
No-one understands when they say that you should
ground yourself.
They do not understand that you are not of land, but of
sea.

Zanzibar

Hurry up my love
The sun is rising and dhows are awaiting upon the shore
Hurry up my love
The sands are shifting and water is yearning
For your heart once more.

The blessing of the sea

Let me feel the sea, behind me and beneath me
Let me not feel the hard edges of life
Or the bitterness of those
Jealous of the freedom that the sea has brought me
Let me sail away
Carried by the wind to wild adventures
To settle quietly on emerald shores where
People with warm smiles await
To greet me.

When your eternal restlessness haunts you like a constant shifting sea.

There is so much beauty in one's own tongue and guess what, you even see the world around you through words. Words do not therefore come from the mouth but also from the heart, eyes and the tongue.

Marchand ambulan (The fast food guy)

Deux la mains deux kote
Mo demande moi si li pas
Pu reste koum sa
Ou pe assiser tranquil tranquil
Ala li vini
Ala li la
So kachara dans deux les bras
La kre kancrela
Medicine lezar
Putu chaud
Pistasse salee
Fer ou chois madame
Pli bon ou pas pu gagne
Bizin paye factures?
Ala 10 lenvelope pu ou
Mette dans sak pu ene lotte zour
Tir plan madame, la vie court
Ene ti balier pu ou la varangue?
Bizin desordre, pu ena lordre
Putu la chaud madame
Pas fine fer hier
Meme si mo fine sorti brisee verdiere
La caz loin madame, prend pistasse
Ramasser madame, mette dans sak
Bus la pas pu sorti astere
Prend, aster madame, pas bizin per!

Ti la Soif (Thirst)

Pa blier to ti la soif
Sa ti di the
Beau grand matin
Goutte ene ti jus
En bas la foire
Bwar alouda
Pas fer grand nwar
Ramasse katora
Alle bord la mer
Tap ene ti grogue
Prend ene ti verre
Soleil pe desann
La nuit pe monter
Les temps pe couler
Degagee, debouler
To ti la soif pe attan
To ti gajak
To famille, to bann.

Manz la Caz (Eating Home)

Gato pima
Gato manioc
Pate poisson salee
Napolitaine
Ti samoosa
Tou c'est ki to kapav penser
Na pa kiter
Battee larguer
Boulette, mi foon, riz cantonnais
Kan to fini, pas oublier
Manz la caz aussi!!!

Poets are funny people, truly they are. Funny in a sad kind of way. They are often on the verge of tears as they start to compose. Few people know that. Here are seven poems filled with light and laughter. If you go through enough Mondays, you can be a poet too.

The Airy and Light Champagne

One flute down...or is that two?
It's hard to tell when you're feeling blue
But who can flee the bubble rise
An ever golden that never dies?
My fingers fly across the keys
I try to beat deadlines with ease
By my side the champagne rests
Company, cheerer, pause and test
Clearly I should not have number three
It is not good for thinking, writing or me
But alas procrastination is my art
So I fill up yet another glass
Verse four you say, surely she must
By now desist, or writing's bust
But that ever golden never dies
It keeps me smiling, writing lies

By my Side

With you by my side
a million Mondays can rise
and I will not fall.

Colour

The sky outside my window
Is the brightest blue
It is married to
The tender green of oaks
Soaking up yellow sunshine

Sunshine

Like sunshine, love falls upon you in the quiet moments.
It's warmth bringing to life all that is still.

Rain-Writer

Heavy drops Pummel
down
Urging words to spill out
and wet dry minds.

My Dear Phone
(Thoughts in a meeting!)

Oh how I wish I'd charged u up
But alas I have forgot
And now as I await the start
Of yet another boring 'fart'
I grasp your fading fingers
And wished I'd made you limber
Through your eyes a thousand stories
Smiles, quips and untold glories
Alas, fool that I am I clean forgot
Your shimmering beauty needs to be charged up.

The Twatterly Twit
(Or how not to be a manager)

To be a twat and a twit is a skill
That the marginally talented can fulfill
For it requires only a few hours
Of twatterly thinking and
Twitterly posturing.
The twit will rise
On twatterabilities
Devoid of truth and all sensibilities
His twitterology quickly spreads
Among the similarly brain dead
His twatterliness knows no bounds
It scythes the wise, the true, the kind
But no one sees such tragedies
To most it seems genuine ingenuity
So, as the true, the kind, the wise fall
The twatterly twit rises ever tall
His labile lips, greasy palms and easy heart
Helps him to play the game, as art.

There is nothing worse than the feeling of dis-belonging. No matter what you do, you will not fit in. Here are two poems on xenophobia in South Africa. The next two speak of ancestral ties for all Africans in the diaspora.

Blackish Woman (an Other poem)

Woman teetering on the end tip of Africa
Caught between living here
Travelling there
Being nowhere
Blackish they say
Not quite us, never us
Your tongue cannot clip
a thousand clicks
You fail at kanala and asseblief
Your roti's dry, weave unkempt
Forever applying to belong
Slipping, missing, falling into
Cracks of exclusion
Paying, calling, fighting wars
that can never be won
Patience is for you, they say
Your kind is good at waiting, begging
Achievement is not enough
Don't be a 'cleva'
Stop expecting favors
Stop expecting reason
Stop expecting ease
Just stop
Learning, thinking, trying all
Day -- you are alone Blackish woman
There's no rescue, for you.

Borders

There are a million borders waiting
For you little one.
The border of the moon, the border of the sun.
The rising of the tide, the wind of the great north
Those borders little one, cannot be overcome.
There are a million borders waiting
In the office down the street.
Where the language that is spoken is not the one you
speak.
There are a million borders waiting
As you write that last exam
And you dream of borders falling
Before a life that must expand
But there a million borders waiting
Behind concrete airport slabs
Those million borders child
Will send you to rehab
Those million borders will stop you,
Will catch you before the prize.
Those million borders baby
Will hasten your demise
You will tango with officials
And waltz with their forms
But no good will come honey
No offers, gifts or money
Those million borders darling
Will make you change your mind
Pack your bags again baby
And leave the borders behind.

The Outsider's Gift

It was late and he hadn't closed shop.
He was remembering how the wind had called his name,
How the sea curled under his feet and
The horizon had beckoned in its blue brilliance,
Promising untold gifts.
Those gifts did not come easily
And they would not come to those waiting on familiar
shores.
So he crossed the open sea
Of thorny shrubs, dunes and hungry goats
Slipped past borders manned by easy guards
And landed in a city some say is paved with gold.
Steadily he began.
With sweets, belts and cigarettes
Building his dream in fine detail.
He was about to pick up his keys
From the hook next to the cigarettes when
A ball of fire hit the stack of newspapers on the floor
It burned through the day's headlines.
As the smoke eased upwards
He saw only their hands
Rough, scarred and twitching with envy
Suddenly he felt his skin
He heard his own tongue
Rattling in his head
Piece by piece they unravelled his dream.
When they were done,
He sat down on the floor
Left with only one gift
All that he had learned.

Dust shall Rise
(an Ode to Maya Angelou)

Ancestors deep
In histories steeped
Melting, writhing, spluttering still
Speak against the world's will
Straighten each spoken lie
Twist and turn those who defy
Destinies foretold, paths defined
Stamp and raise dust above the sky
Cry the highest shrillest cry
Behold your slave child is near
The one for centuries held dear
No hair on her head shall they take
No breath will leave her by mistake
On no path will she stumble
Her feet are guided by your dusty hands
Though she doubts, you persist
Wading through dense fields of time
You cannot resist
Your path is tightly wound to hers
Pull yourselves up into the world
Groan and cry till you are heard
Nothing shall stop you
Not war, not lies, not fire
To be for her, is your desire.

Ropes

Invisible ropes
Woven by those who went before
Bound them across oceans deep
But upright men in uniforms crisp
Berets bright with lies
Looked them in the eye
And said this was not so
'You are dark strangers.
Too far gone
Divided by history

They are clanless, landless, rootless
Floating on the thinnest crust of identity'.
But, in the silence of the darkest night
In the densest forest of their minds
By the wet redness of blood
That flows beneath the skin
They saw the ropes
Cords freshly beating still
Untouched by the past
Buried beneath ancient soil
To which they both belonged.

The ropes sensed them near
And writhed in delight
It bid them to lock eyes
To dance
To rekindle the fire of oneness
But the lies were too bright
The lying men too upright
Brimming with greed

Unaware of the need
To tie the ropes once more
To bring the children
Back to shore.

Unmoored, the ropes unravelled
Wisdom floated out to sea
What those who went before knew
Sank to the depths below.

On enchanted isles afar
The children sang
Long, woeful songs
They danced and played
In the fiercest sunlight
Filled with unquenchable sadness.

In many societies, the kite offers powerful imagery. In my society, the kite is often associated with a woman who is uncontrolled, a woman not afraid to speak her mind or follow her dreams. There are references to the rope snapping and the woman going wild. For me, the kite is something that desires to fly, to reach unknown stratospheres. It is fragile, beautiful, precious and misunderstood. Here are two pieces, in which I weave a story of the Little Kite. I think there are still many more stories of the Little Kite!

Gazbia Sirry (Egypt). The Kite. 2009.
https://www.metmuseum.org/toah/hd/egma/hd_egma.htm

Be Yourself little Kite

The wind is here to toss you up
Into a blackened sky.
Flimsy, your ribbon arms are lifted high
Weighted hands
Lengthened rope
Steady eyes
Fix your path across the sky.
Slip through fingers!
Unknot ties!
Do not look behind or down
Flee across the wildest wilds
And be yourself, little kite.

Little Kite and the Butterfly

The little kite floats over the trees
She notices how it feels to be free
In the wide expanse of the sky
In the coldness of the air above
But dark clouds gather, a storm begins
The little kite is soaked to the skin
A harsh wind, emboldened by thunder
Pushes her down, deep and under
The little kite begins to think
'Perhaps I should have been less free'
'Perhaps I should not have been me'
'I should not have unknotted those ties
That kept me tethered to the ground
I should have let the little people fight
Over their little thoughts and little rights.'
As the little kite wept a sorrowful cry
Along came a butterfly
Its gossamer wings sparkling with rain
The butterfly did not have much to say
It crept under the sodden kite
now lying in mud and soil below
It listened to the kite and all her sorrows,
her dreams and wishes for tomorrow
As the kite breathed its last
The butterfly closed its eyes
For days, the butterfly remained
under the kite, in the pouring rain
Then one day, the rain stopped
The butterfly, wings dry
Took to the skies.

I am secretly obsessed with art. Although I am supposed to be a serious writer, I sometimes run away and hide in paintings, chase literature and dance with the stars. Obviously, I do this when no one is looking, how can I lead others and be frivolous at the same time?

If

If you could run away
to the place where dreams could not find you
Would you?
If you could escape
the rough ropes of obligation
tying your mind to the ground
Would you?
If you could throw off the heavy cloak of duty
Would you?
If you could say no more to the politics of inwardness
Would you?
Would you run off into the starry night of van Gogh?
Sleep under Gaugin's pandanus tree?
Hide behind Caravaggio in yet another portentous scene
Roam through Matthee's green forest
Skip behind Kentridge while his pen runs riot?
Would you scream along with Maya
As she yells why the Caged Bird Sings
Follow Morisson through twisted words of love
And laugh with Salinger over the absurdity of war?

Would you weep over Naipaul's bloodied Bend of River
Bend time with Dali and dance with Fred
While Ginger is not looking?
Would you agree with Okri that Africa is not as it seems?
Would you wish away Martel's anguished ocean crossing
That deep lonely known only to mythical boys and tigers
locked in one another's company?
Truth is, there is no art which will have you
Nothing is ready for the unusual brilliance that burns
within

The canvas remains unmoved
Words are stilled
Authors hide behind their narrative, stiff, unthinking
Tied to borders which others have set
So even if you would, chances are, they would not.

Here are two poems about the mundane and quite possibly the lot of many women. I am washing plates but somehow the domestic scene is interrupted by a desire to be at one with my books. So great is this desire that in a real dream, my dogs come to the rescue and wash the plates for me.

Sinking

Standing by, looking on
I see gray water out of which arise
Spoons, cups and one soaked fry
Faint memories of unfettered hands pierce through
Reminding me of the everythingness of having nothing
to do
To the side I see the books I need to read
Authors who never curtsied for
Plates, cups, spoons and floors
Men, children or Others-in-law
I yearn to trip over their sentences
To slip through paragraphs
And plunge into chapters
To be submerged in words
To watch the chaos from below
But here I am by the sink
Wrist deep in duties known
Chores repeat and never cease
For a house
Can never be appeased...

The Dream

You were baking
In a shop full of bread
People bustled in
Coins dropped
Tills clanged
In the background
A warm-eared dog
Without apron
Washed plates
Its paws sodden with soapy suds

I have a dream

I have a dream to float, like a leaf on the blue
I have a dream to taste the saltiest wave lapping
against a grainy shore
I have a dream to sit, knee deep in the sand wrapping
my mind around stories untold
I have a dream to sleep under humid skies sighing
in the loneliness that only the field can bring
I have a dream
But the dream does not wish to have me.

The level of violence against women has become intolerable. I wrote this poem for Nene, a young South African woman brutally killed this past year. Reference to the 'cords lie fresh and beating still', appear in this and another poem in the collection. It refers to the vigour of a young soul, whose umbilical cord lies fresh in ancestral soil. The dreadful trauma of violence is that it denies its victims the opportunity to be ordinary. To live a life like everyone else – to be a dry autumn leaf whose passing we do not notice. Rest in peace Nene.

True (a tribute to Nene)

True. Ordinariness is impossible these days
To flit without thought
Mindless like a dry autumn leaf unnoticed,
A leaf loosened by a knotted tree
Hurried along by the most unexpected breeze.
We do not mourn its dry auburn hue
Disappearing into the distance.
But green leaves with veins so true
ripped from a rooted tree
Are not free
Beneath the cords lie fresh and beating still
Expecting dreams to be fulfilled
The tree bleeds and the forest cries
for ordinariness denied.

Refugee Woman

In the early morning
She rises from the cardboard bed.
Her child is hungry but there is last night's bread.
The street is cold in the morning
But it's better than fields of blood
The street is dark in the morning
But it's better than the rifles snout
The street is full of men in the morning
But they're better than the ones who --
The street is wide in the morning
And that's enough, for her, for two.

Club Horror

There was nothing quite like the club
That place where white people had fun
That place where uncle Bom played the piano
And everyone drank gin and tonic
There was nothing quite like the club
Where we all learned to swim
Properly mind you, three strokes one breath
There was nothing like the club
Even bodies floated down the river beside it.

Big Bertha (The factory)

Black flecks of burnt cane raining down
Steam from the river, rising to her crown
Smoke from Big Bertha, her stacks so high
Squeezing that sugar with her steely thighs
Sweet scent of molasses filling the sky
Children dancing like flowers wild
Men feeding her boilers dry
Dust in their hair, nose and eyes
Big Bertha, loving tough mother
Let no man fall and no child cry
She stood proud, her head held high
Black molasses beauty, undenied.

Cesaria

Velvet is her voice
Deep in island sorrow
Her yearning sings
Like wildfire
Burning memories
Filling displaced minds
With smoke and ash
scattered into the sea
Floating into the vast blue
It reaches inside you
And tells of your past
Rising from the deep.

Cesaria Evora is a mournful, soulful singer from the windswept island of Cap Verde. I can easily say that I have listened to her songs many times over. I have written books with her voice in my head.

With Him

With Him
She walked on paths unknown
Followed twisted rivers riddled with gossiping pebbles
With Him
She trudged through forests dense with branchless
decisions
She crossed deserts of unending patience
And with Him
Bruised and uncertain
She witnessed the glorious sun rising
And watched a sparrow fly free
She stood at the shore
And saw fish bend a bow's edge
She walked with Him
Through a world
Filled with dark foreboding pall
With Him, her soul grew wildflowers
And covered fields with gold.

I wrote this one during a lecture on philosophy as laughter

Seeds of laughter

Laughter says the philosopher
Feeds the unknowing, truthful life
We consume it and it, us
So, crack open the fresh delight of a child
Let it's simple yellow yolk run freely into your smile
Drink freely of sweet power
And stumble about, drunken with the joy of petty
superiority
Face the abyss, belly full of uncertainty
Let fear consume you
Deep down, in the dark unknown where nothing grows
Release the lion laughter
And mock the seedless drought
Only then will you will return, glowing
Like the fertile sun on a forsaken land.

When I heard Fela Kuti's Zombie, I couldn't resist. See if you can spot Org Redesign in here.

Zombie
(in honour of Fela Kuti)

No thinkin'
No blinkin'
Just shufflin'
Stumblin'
To blunt order
Fulfillin'
Redesign
Scrambling over
Your lawn
Coming
To get u
Groaning
Supurating
Liquifying
Bloodied flesh
Rot overflowing
No thinkin'
No blinkin'
Ate your dog
Too late now
Blunted stare
Hanging eye
Staring
Your way
Sees you
Too late now

Give in
Be eaten
It's war.

Dance with Me

Dance with me said the sun
My light will keep you warm
When the bitter wind inches you
To the edge and bids you fall.
Dance with me said the moon
As I light up the dark
If shadows fall upon you
I will shine upon your path.
Dance with me, said the dawn
I bring hope and new delight
With me, no tears shall follow
And your days will be bright.
She graciously thanked them
For their kindness unsurpassed,
Picked up her dancing shoes
And danced alone, at last.

Then I came to the end. I let the words set me down.

The Journey

Bravely she started on a journey
The end of which she could not see
It seemed as if this journey
Required skill, ability, tenacity
Others told her she would suffer if
She did not listen to her betters
She would break if
She did not bend to those in power
Silently, quietly she knitted the days
And months and years, into
A warm blanket of care and love
She made a bed of comfort
She furnished a room of peace
And built a house of inspiration
All who passed by found their dreams
And these grew like wildflowers on fields unclaimed
Blossoming into art, thought and argument.
When she finally folded up the blanket
Closed the door and hung up the keys
She realized that the journey
Was different to what she had been told
It was not a journey of skill, ability, tenacity
It was not a journey of listening to betters
Nor was it about bending to those in power
It was a journey of seeing others' dreams
And seeking to make those, reality.

Expectations

I am tired of expectations she said,
The desires of others shed upon my path
Like pine needles on a barren forest floor.
Dry under the feet, they bear no resemblance
To the green foliage that rises to the sky.
In the darkness made by upright trunks
The buds of thoughts desiring to be free
Are nowhere to be found,
Only the seeds of others
and their weeds of propriety.
Below their roots coil through dry soil
Choking tender shoots rising to meet the sun.

No one is here to cut down that forest.
It shuts out all light from the sky.

I am tired of expectations she said
And with that,
She walked out from under the forest
And into the clearing.
The light of the sun dazzled her
The air took her breath away,
Flowers with bending stems surrounded her
A clear stream beckoned
Teeming with fish, dancing in the cold.

Printed in the United States
By Bookmasters